Piano Time Dance

Pauline Hall

MUSIC DEPARTMENT

OXFORD
UNIVERSITY PRESS

OXFORD
UNIVERSITY PRESS

Great Clarendon Street, Oxford OX2 6DP, England

Oxford University Press is a department of the University of Oxford.
It furthers the University's aim of excellence in research, scholarship,
and education by publishing worldwide

Oxford is a registered trade mark of Oxford University Press
in the UK and in certain other countries

13

ISBN 978–0–19–337005–0

Illustrations by Andy Hammond
Music and text origination by
Katie Johnston
Printed in Great Britain on acid-free paper by
Halstan & Co. Ltd., Amersham, Bucks.

With thanks to Jan Bullard for advising on piece selection and fingering.

Contents

Hoofer's Delight

A 'hoofer' is a tap dancer. Many of the early hoofers started their careers by dancing on street corners, in cities across America.

Philip Croydon

Earthy, with swing

Allemande

The allemande was an elegant dance that probably came from Germany. It was popular during the late seventeenth century.

Claude Gervaise (*fl.*1540–60)
arr. Alan Bullard

Needles and Pins

This is an example of a Morris dance, a cheerful English folk dance that is performed by groups of dancers carrying sticks and wearing costumes decorated with flowers and bells.

Melody anon.
arr. Alan Bullard

Chatterbox Charlie

This dance is a calypso, a style that comes from the West Indies. The calypso is often used in Caribbean Carnivals, and the music includes steel drums.

Paul Drayton

Forget-me-not Waltz

A waltz is a ballroom dance that was fashionable in Vienna two hundred years ago and is still popular today.

Stephen Duro

Hornpipe

The hornpipe was danced by sailors in the days of the old sailing ships.

Pauline Hall

Bright and breezy

Gigue à l'Angloise

The French gigue is a lively and energetic dance that is sometimes known as a jig. The title of this piece means 'gigue in the English style'.

Georg Philipp Telemann (1681–1767)
arr. Pauline Hall

Ch-ch-chilly Cha-cha-cha

The cha-cha-cha is a 1950s ballroom dance that takes its name from its distinctive rhythm. Here, the staccatos give the music a chilly and shivery feel.

Paul Drayton

Very crisp and shivery

Gavotte from Trio Sonata in D, Op. 5 No. 2 HWV 397

Originally a lively French folk dance, the gavotte later became an elegant dance that was popular at the French royal court.

George Frideric Handel (1685–1759)
ed. Maisie Aldridge

Perfect Polka

Originally from Bohemia, the polka is an energetic dance in 2/4 time.

David Cullen

'Clog Dance' from the ballet La fille mal gardée

Imagine having to dance to this music wearing wooden clogs! For the tapping bars, tap with your knuckles on the piano lid.

Peter Ludwig Hertel (1817–99)
arr. Pauline Hall

Latin Moves

This is an example of a rumba, a Latin American dance originally from Cuba. It is usually accompanied by percussion instruments such as claves and maracas.

Alan Haughton

Sarabande from Keyboard Suite No. 4 in D minor HWV 437

The sarabande is a slow, stately dance in three time. Notice that this sarabande is in 3/2 time, which means that you count three minims in each bar.

George Frideric Handel (1685–1759)
arr. Pauline Hall

Festival Mazurka

The mazurka is a dance from Poland with accented rhythms that mimic the movements of the dancers.

Alan Bullard

Minuet from Keyboard Sonata No. 5 in G Hob. XVI:11

The minuet is a graceful French dance in three time. It was popular in the royal courts of seventeenth-century France.

Joseph Haydn (1732–1809)
arr. Pauline Hall

Tango Misterio

The tango is a dramatic dance from Argentina. 'Misterio' is the Spanish word for mystery.

Nikki Iles

Blue Train

This swing dance is in the blues style and should feel very relaxed and laid-back.

David Cullen

The Soft-shoe Shuffle

The soft-shoe shuffle is danced using steps from the tap dance. Instead of wearing metal-soled tap shoes, the dancer wears shoes with soft soles.

Nikki Iles

The Trot of Mr Fox

The foxtrot is a gliding ballroom dance that was one of the most popular dances of the 1920s and 1930s.

David Cullen

Circle Dance

This piece is in the style of an eastern European folk dance often performed at weddings. The bride sits on a raised chair while the guests dance around her in a circle, with the music getting faster and faster.

Nikki Iles

Disco Baroque

Disco dominated popular music during the late 1970s. Using similar sequences to those found in earlier music, this piece suggests the rhythmic disco feel with a steady drum beat, which should be maintained (in your head!) in the middle section.

Alan Bullard

Aces High

Anthony Marks

Aces High

This is an example of reggae, a popular music style that originated in Jamaica and has strong off-beats.

Anthony Marks

Relaxed and steady

Two-tone Tango

Paul Drayton

Two-tone Tango

This is another Latin American tango.

Paul Drayton

Amber's Samba

David Cullen

Amber's Samba

The samba is a lively dance from Brazil that often features in Carnival parades.

David Cullen